MVFOL

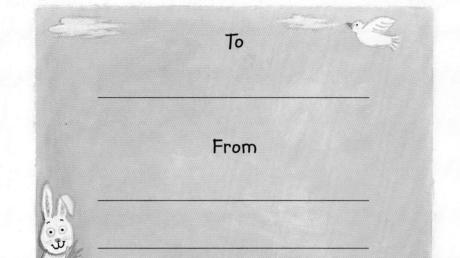

To

_____

From

_____

_____

To Celia L.R.

To Mark L.P.

Text by Lois Rock
Illustrations copyright © 1999 Liz Pichon
This edition copyright © 1999 Lion Publishing

The moral rights of the author and illustrator
have been asserted

Published by
Lion Publishing
4050 Lee Vance View, Colorado Springs,
CO 80918, USA
ISBN 0 7459 4093 5

First edition 1995
Revised edition 1999
This US edition 2000
10 9 8 7 6 5 4 3 2 1 0

Acknowledgments
The wording of the Ten Commandments at the end of this book has been adapted
from the version printed in *The Revised Standard Version* of the Bible, copyright © 1946,
1952, 1971 by the Division of Christian Education of the National Council of the
Churches of Christ in the USA. Used by permission.

Library of Congress CIP data applied for

Typeset in 20/30 Baskerville BT
Printed and bound in Singapore

The
Ten Commandments
for Children

Words by Lois Rock
Pictures by Liz Pichon

LION
Children's Books

The Ten Commandments

In this book are ten great sayings called commandments. They are very old. The story is that long ago the great Maker God gave people these Ten Commandments so they would know the good and right way to live their lives.

I am God.
I always take care of my people.
I am the One whom you should love
and respect.

Who made the world?
Who filled it with good things?

Who made people to live in it
and be happy?

Is there a Great Maker God,
who takes care of all there is?

Is there a Great Maker God,
who knows what is wise?

In all that is around me,
may I glimpse the Maker.

Do not let anything be more important than God.

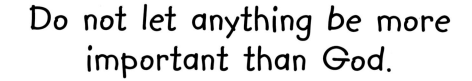

So many things can seem important:

chasing after fun;

buying wonderful things;

having everything go your own way.

But many wise people have found that
the good things of this world only
bring happiness when people
remember the God who made them all.

Let me discover what
is truly important.

Take care how you speak about God.

 It is easy to say that you know what is right.

 It is easy to say that you know what is wrong.

 It is easy to say that you know what must be done.

 It is easy to boast about what you will do.

But are you greater and wiser than the Maker God? If you are not, take care what you say.

Let me learn to speak wisely of the Maker God.

Keep one day of rest each week, as God first planned.

From the beginning
God made times of
work and times of rest:

Let all that must be
done fill six busy days,
and leave the seventh
day for rest and joy.

Let me learn when to be
busy, and when to rest.

Show respect to your mother and father.

Each tiny baby,
each growing child
needs the love and help
of their family.

Each tiny baby,
each growing child
can give love and help
to their family.

Then happiness can grow as everyone learns to find their own place in the world.

Let me be part of a loving family.

Do not kill.

Alive means growing,
changing, learning,
loving and finding
delight in all that the
world has to give.

It is the Maker God
who gives life.
It is not for people
to take life away.

Let me *be* gentle with others,
and cherish every life.

Husbands and wives:
Keep your special love just for each other.

Husbands and wives promise
to be special friends for ever;
to be loyal;
to be kind;
to be special to each other.
It is a promise that guards
the love they share.

Let promises be kept,

so love can grow.

Do not steal.

The world is the home
that all people share.
Each person deserves
to have what they need
to live in happiness.

Let me respect what
belongs to others.

Do not tell lies that get others into trouble.

Lies, whispering,
tales that are not true:

they bring sadness and
pain, loneliness and tears,

and divide people
from one another.

When people look for what is true and
good in each other, everyone can grow
to be the best that they can be.

Let me speak words that are true.

Do not be greedy for the things other people have.

God made a world that can
give everyone all they need.
Do not look greedily at what
others have.
Enjoy what is given to you.

Let me be happy with
what is given to me.

The Ten Commandments appear in the ancient books of the people of Israel, the Jews. These books were written between two and three thousand years ago in the language of the people, called Hebrew. Hundreds of years ago, they were collected together; the collection of books is the Jewish Bible, and the Old Testament of the Christian Bible.

This book tells the Ten Commandments in simple words. On the next page you will see the commandments again, this time using English words based closely on the Hebrew words.

They mention things of long ago: the story of God helping the people to escape from Egypt, where they had been slaves; the problem of people forgetting God, and instead making 'graven images'—carvings of other beings that they imagined to be gods.

The underlying message remains clear: people are to love God and one another, for this is the good and right way to live.

These Ten Commandments belong both to the Jewish people and to Christians, who share the same background of stories.

All over the world, people from many other backgrounds respect them as part of the world's heritage of wisdom.

God spoke all these words, saying, I am the Lord your God, who brought you out of the land of Egypt… You shall have no other gods before me.

You shall not make for yourself graven images… you shall not bow down to them or serve them…

You shall not take the name of the Lord your God in vain.

Remember the sabbath day, to keep it holy.

Honour your father and your mother.

You shall not kill.

You shall not commit adultery.

You shall not steal.

You shall not bear false witness against your neighbour.

You shall not covet anything that is your neighbour's.